# Running Through the Bible

**by**

**Chris Wright**



Paperback ISBN: 978-0-9927642-6-5
Available as an e-Book ISBN: 978-0-9933941-3-3



PUBLISHED BY
WHITE TREE PUBLISHING
BRISTOL
UNITED KINGDOM

wtpbristol@gmail.com

# Author's Note ( see books on back page)

Due to copyright restrictions, it is not possible to quote from just a single translation of the Bible in this book. Selecting two translations has not been easy, because many people have a favourite translation, maybe one that they believe to be the most reliable or easiest to understand.

I have chosen two English translations widely used today: the New International Version (NIV), and the English Standard Version (ESV). The version used in each quote is marked with its Bible reference at the end of every chapter.

I am not suggesting that other translations are inferior in any way. Please feel free to look up the references in your own Bible. I support a statement from the introduction of the King James (Authorised) Bible of 1611 – a translation still widely used and loved today – where the translators state: *We do not deny, nay we affirm and avow, that the very meanest [poorest] translation of the Bible in English, set forth by men of our profession [professing our faith] . . . containeth the word of God, nay, is the word of God.*

Here are a few suggestions for going deeper. (There are, of course, many other sources.) Visit *www.ewordtoday.com* for free online Bible reading plans, in several languages, including *The Bible in One Year* with 365 readings arranged in chronological order starting on any date you choose. Reading plans are on *www.biblegateway.com.* See also *www.youversion.com* for hundreds of free Bible versions in many languages online.

*www.cwr.org.uk* and *www.scriptureunion.org.uk* are just two publishers of daily Bible-reading notes and other useful study material. You will also benefit from a Bible commentary – expensive, but probably a lot cheaper than your phone, tablet or sports kit! If you need help in choosing the most appropriate reading material for yourself, ask your church leader or a Christian bookshop for advice.

# Chapter 1

Let me start with a word of warning. If you're in church, and someone at the front asks for hands up from anyone who's read the whole book of Hezekiah, don't be tempted to put your hand up. It's an old trick. There *is* no book of Hezekiah!

Yes, Hezekiah appears in the Bible. He's a significant person, and we can read one of his prayers, but he didn't write a whole book. Is he:

A great-grandson of Adam and Eve?

A disbelieving uncle of Noah, when God decided to start again with people in the Flood?

A wise servant of Abraham and Sarah, the couple chosen by God to become the ancestors of the people later called the Children of Israel?

One of Jacob's grandsons when the Children of Israel were slaves in Egypt?

A priest who made a golden calf in the desert of Sinai, in defiance of Moses when they escaped from Egypt in the Exodus?

A scheming servant of Samuel, in the time of the Judges that came after Moses?

A priest who blessed King David before a major victory over the Philistines?

A writer of several Psalms?

A prophet who warned King Solomon that his kingdom would be divided in two: Israel with the city of Samaria in the north, and Judah with the city of Jerusalem in the south?

A godly but eventually unwise king who was stupid enough to proudly show the treasures of his palace in Jerusalem to the visiting Babylonians, and not worry about the consequences?

A prophet who later promised the Jews in exile, captured by the Babylonians, that they would one day return to Jerusalem?

A skilled stone mason who helped Nehemiah rebuild Jerusalem and the Temple, seventy years after the Babylonians had destroyed it for the treasures?

A priest in the Temple in Jerusalem who announced the birth of Jesus, the promised Messiah?

A prominent Pharisee who argued with Jesus about Jesus' power and authority to forgive sins?

One of the first men to see Jesus after he rose from the dead after the crucifixion?

A leader of the early Christian church in Antioch?

A scribe who helped the apostle Paul, who was in prison, copy some of his letters to the new churches?

The leader of a failing church condemned by Jesus in the book of Revelation?

We'll find Hezekiah later, but you may be surprised to know that in these few questions we've raced through the Bible from beginning to end, with major events in their correct order, even though Hezekiah was only there for one of them.

If you skimmed through the list because you already know the answer, read it again, carefully this time. You may find you learn a lot from it.

I can't promise that there will be answers in these pages that will help you shine in the obligatory Bible question(s) at your local quiz night, but if you're new to the Bible, I want to give you a clearer idea of the events between its pages.

# Chapter 2

The Bible is a massive book and it should be read slowly and carefully – and of course prayerfully. So why are we running through it? Why the rush?

The Bible isn't like a long novel that you pick up to take on holiday, where you start at the beginning and work your way through to the end in just a few days. It's a collection of writings, individual books that took many centuries to put together. The first book, Genesis, records events at the beginning of time and quickly moves on to people who lived several thousand years ago. The last book, Revelation, was written near the end of the first century AD.

All I want to do now is give a flavour of what's between the start of Genesis in the Old Testament, and the end of Revelation in the New Testament. This should help you get to grips with reading it with more understanding.

As you will probably, but not necessarily, know, the Old Testament is the story of God's people before the birth of Jesus. The New Testament tells the birth, life, death and resurrection of Jesus, the Son of God, with writing by leaders of the early Christian church.

If you want to start reading at Genesis chapter 1, that's fine. But if you keep going, you'll soon come to chapter after chapter of names and regulations. Most people new to the Bible quickly lose interest at this point, wrongly assuming that this is the shape of things to come. If they understood the Bible better, they would know which parts are more interesting.

I'm saying more interesting, not more important. Christians believe that the whole Bible is the word of God, so every bit of it is important. But much of it is not for newcomers or the faint-hearted to dip into.

So to give this flavour and basic understanding of the Bible, I'm taking verses from various books of the Bible and sometimes abridging them considerably. All direct quotations from the Bible will be in italics. The missing wording will be indicated by ellipses. There will be a letter for an endnote after the Bible readings in italics, where you will find the reference to the full reading at the end of each chapter. The references are often for longer readings than the quoted words. I recommend you read every reference in full later, as a way of getting a better insight of the Bible. Let's start at the very beginning, at Genesis chapter 1.

*In the beginning God created the heavens and the earth. . . . And God said, "Let there be light," and there was light.*[a]

Later, we read: *Then God said, "Let us make man in our image, in our likeness, and let them rule over the fish of the sea and the birds of the air, over the livestock, over all the earth, and over all the creatures that move along the ground."* [b]

Then at the end of chapter 1: *God saw all that he had made, and it was very good.*[c]

When God created Adam and Eve — the first people with souls and the ability to know and love God — everything was very good. If God thought it was all very good, then it was. God also gave people free will, allowing them to live a perfect life with him — or go their own way. Probably everyone knows, or can guess, what happens next.

In Genesis 3 it all starts to go wrong. Satan, the enemy of God who was once an angel of light, chose to disobey God and set up his own powerbase with other rebellious angels. Here, he appears as a snake:

*Now the serpent was more crafty than any of the wild animals the LORD God had made. He said to the woman, "Did God really say, 'You must not eat from any tree in the garden'?"*

*The woman said to the serpent, "We may eat fruit from the trees in the garden, but God did say, 'You must not eat fruit from the tree that is in the middle of the garden, and you must not touch it, or you will die.'"*

*"You will not surely die," the serpent said to the woman. "For God knows that when you eat of it your eyes will be opened, and you will be like God, knowing good and evil."* [d]

Having their own way seemed like a good idea at the time, but after disobeying God, Adam and Eve feel ashamed and afraid. When God confronts them, they start the blame game.

*The man said, "The woman you put here with me — she gave me some fruit from the tree, and I ate it."*

*Then the LORD God said to the woman, "What is this you have done?"*

*The woman said, "The serpent deceived me, and I ate."*

*So the LORD God said to the serpent, "Because you have done this, cursed are you above all the livestock and all the wild animals! You will crawl on your belly and you will eat dust all the days of your life. And I will put enmity between you and the woman, and between your offspring and hers; he will crush your head, and you will strike his heel."*

*To the woman he said, "I will greatly increase your pains in childbearing; with pain you will give birth to children. Your desire will be for your husband, and he will rule over you."*

*To Adam he said, "Because you listened to your wife and ate from the tree about which I commanded you, 'You must not eat of it,' Cursed is the ground because of you; through painful toil you will eat of it all the days of your life.*

*"It will produce thorns and thistles for you, and you will eat the plants of the field. By the sweat of your brow you will eat your food until you return to the ground, since from it you were taken; for dust you are and to dust you will return."* [e]

I've quoted these verses at length, because it's important to see that although at the start everything was very good, it is people who quickly went wrong. And it's our selfish way of living that is causing so much pain and suffering today. This is *not* how God planned it, but he allowed it rather than create us as divinely-controlled robots. He wanted them to love him voluntarily, and according to the Bible he still does.

*God shows his love for us in that while we were still sinners, Christ died for us.*[f]

This is just one of many, many verses in both the Old and New Testaments about God's love for us, and it is the red cord that will run through the Bible from start to finish. Red – the colour of blood. God says that Satan, the devil, will be crushed by the "seed" of a woman – we now know that woman to be the Virgin Mary. Her son Jesus is the seed, the offspring. If you're not at all familiar with the Bible, this comes at the start of the New Testament with the birth of Jesus Christ, the Son of God. Christians believe that Jesus overcame death at his crucifixion. When Jesus rose from the dead, Satan was defeated. But we're getting ahead of ourselves here. Let's see what happens next.

---

[a] Genesis 1:1-26 (NIV)
[b] Genesis 1:26 (NIV)
[c] Genesis 1:31 (NIV)
[d] Genesis 3:1-5 (NIV)
[e] Genesis 3:12-19 (NIV)
[f] Romans 5:8 (NIV)

## SUGGESTIONS ON HOW TO READ THE BIBLE

When you read about an event in the Bible, try to imagine you're actually there. What's happening? What is everyone thinking? How are they dressed? How old are the main characters? Is it sunny or raining? Hot or cold? Night or day? This will help you get a better idea of what is going on – even if you imagine some details incorrectly. You need to *be* there, watching and listening. And be sure to watch out for that red cord.

As soon as you feel ready to go deeper, ask the Holy Spirit to reveal more of God in the pages. Although God can speak to us through individual verses (sometimes verses taken completely out of context), it is better to read whole passages, and see what God is telling us through them, rather than regularly taking a "lucky dip". True understanding of God and his plans for us come from the whole Bible, although we will surely need the help of good Bible teaching.

Bible reading notes, with a passage and thought for each day, are a great way to read the Bible. Ask your church or a Christian bookshop for help in finding the best notes for your age and understanding of the Bible. In other words, some Bible reading notes are simpler or more detailed than others. The choice is yours. See my Author's Note.

# Chapter 3

Adam and Eve are not only thrown out of the Garden of Eden, where there has been complete safety and a daily walk with God, they have to put up with problems with their two sons, Cain and Abel. After an argument about which of them brought the better sacrifice to God, Cain ends up killing Abel.

From then on, for several generations, it's mostly downhill for these early people who are not living in the way in which God created them. Eventually God decides that enough is enough. He will start again with a godly man called Noah, along with his family. Yes, it's the story of Noah and the ark.

*The LORD saw how great man's wickedness on the earth had become, and that every inclination of the thoughts of his heart was only evil all the time. The LORD was grieved that he had made man on the earth, and his heart was filled with pain. . . . But Noah found favour in the eyes of the LORD. . . . Noah was a righteous man, blameless among the people of his time, and he walked with God. . . . God said to Noah, "I am going to put an end to all people, for the earth is filled with violence because of them. I am surely going to destroy both them and the earth. So make yourself an ark of cypress wood; make rooms in it and coat it with pitch inside and out. . . . I will establish my covenant with you, and you will enter the ark — you and your sons and your wife and your sons' wives with you. . . . Noah did everything just as God commanded him.*[a]

The flood comes and Noah and his family are safe. Many months later the ark comes to rest and the sun shines. God points to the rainbow and says it stands for a promise that he will never do the same again.

Although Noah wouldn't have known it at the time, the red cord is running through this event, for just as there was safety in the ark, so there is safety in the promised Messiah (Jesus Christ) who will come to earth several thousand years later, the descendant of Eve.

Then: *The nations spread out over the earth after the flood.* God had instructed Noah to do this with his family and their descendants, but unfortunately they didn't get far. In Babel they stopped and built a tall tower to prove that they were important and could reach heaven – which of course they couldn't manage to do. *So the LORD scattered them . . . over all the earth.*[b]

When did the events in the Bible happen? In the middle of the seventeenth century, Archbishop James Ussher decided to put some dates into Bible events, and these appear at the top of pages of some older Bibles, both Catholic and Protestant translations. However, they are definitely not part of the original writing, and many of them are now considered wrong.

Archaeologists, geologists and Bible scholars today are coming up with dates that are more reliable than those from earlier researchers. But with some events, such as when Moses was in Egypt, they are still at odds with each other by many years – centuries even. So, interesting though it would be to know exactly when various people lived in the early chapters of the Old Testament, it's not essential that we know, and certainly not worth any bitter disputes. Nowhere in the Bible does it say that a correct understanding of chronology is essential to salvation!

Most Bible scholars are generally in close agreement with the dates from King David onwards (c1000 BC), because the names of many people and places coincide with non-biblical records from surrounding countries.

Most people are familiar with the stages of civilization called the Neolithic, Bronze and Iron Ages. Many used to think that these people were extremely primitive, but modern archaeologists have shown us just how advanced many of them were, by studying recent finds of their pottery, art and ornaments. These ages were also taking place in what we now call the Middle East, but generally happening earlier than the dates of these ages in Europe. Even though one age tended to blur into another, the arrival of advanced technology can be traced from area to area, giving rise to the occasional major advance in civilization.

Early examples of Bronze Age people in the Middle East are Abraham and Sarah. Bible scholars usually date them to around 2000 BC. In a large museum you are likely to find items from the Bronze Age from your local region. In national museums such as the British Museum in London, there are whole displays of amazing goods from what is now Israel and the surrounding countries. These people were certainly not as primitive as once thought.

I find it interesting to speculate what must have been happening in the Bible lands when Stonehenge was built in England, when a local Bronze Age burial mound was first used, and when Iron Age fortifications seen on holiday were built.

If you want to investigate perceived dates of early Bible events for yourself, be prepared to encounter people with *very* strongly held opinions that are not open to negotiation. I take the view that knowing dates is interesting to me as a Bible reader, but things happened when they happened, and no amount of arguing will make them happen at any other time. The Bible sets out to tell the story of God and his plan for us. It is not a dated calendar or science handbook, and we should not try to make it one.

---

[a] Genesis 5:1-32 (NIV)

[b] Genesis 10:32 to 11:9 (NIV)

# Chapter 4

At the top of the previous page, I mentioned Abraham and Sarah. They are the founders of the Jewish race. A great nation is promised for the future. The red cord runs through here.

*The LORD had said to Abram, "Leave your country, your people and your father's household and go to the land I will show you. I will make you into a great nation and I will bless you; I will make your name great, and you will be a blessing. I will bless those who bless you, and whoever curses you I will curse; and all peoples on earth will be blessed through you." So Abram left, as the LORD had told him; and Lot went with him.*[a]

Lot is Abram's nephew. Abram? Yes, it is later that God changes Abram's name to Abraham. Abraham means Father of a Multitude — the father of the promised great nation.

But things don't seem to be working out. Abraham and Sarah are getting older and older, and still no child. Eventually, after an encounter with Three Visitors: *The LORD was gracious to Sarah as he had said, and the LORD did for Sarah what he had promised. Sarah became pregnant and bore a son to Abraham in his old age, at the very time God had promised him. Abraham gave the name Isaac to the son Sarah bore him.*[b]

We really have to hurry on now, but you can read much more about Abraham in the Bible — including God's test of Abraham's faith by asking him to sacrifice his son, in a country where child sacrifice to foreign gods was not unusual.[c]

Isaac marries Rebekah,[d] and they have twin sons Jacob and Esau. Esau is born first:

*Isaac was sixty years old when Rebekah gave birth to them. The boys grew up, and Esau became a skilful hunter, a man of the open country, while Jacob was a quiet man, staying among the tents. . . . Once when Jacob was cooking some stew, Esau came in from the open country, famished. He said to Jacob,*

*"Quick, let me have some of that red stew! I'm famished!" Jacob replied, "First sell me your birthright."*

*"Look, I am about to die," Esau said. "What good is the birthright to me?"*

*But Jacob said, "Swear to me first."*

*So he swore an oath to him, selling his birthright to Jacob. Then Jacob gave Esau some bread and some lentil stew. He ate and drank, and then got up and left. So Esau despised his birthright.*[e]

There is now a time of famine, and Isaac and Rebekah are looking to move on.

*The LORD appeared to Isaac and said, "Do not go down to Egypt; live in the land where I tell you to live. Stay in this land for a while, and I will be with you and will bless you. For to you and your descendants I will give all these lands and will confirm the oath I swore to your father Abraham. I will make your descendants as numerous as the stars in the sky and will give them all these lands, and through your offspring all nations on earth will be blessed, because Abraham obeyed me and kept my requirements, my commands, my decrees and my laws."*[f]

Jacob, now also called Israel, wrestles with God one night, then goes to make peace with his brother Esau.[g] Jacob has twelve sons (the children of Israel, aka Jacob), but his favourite is Joseph. Joseph's jealous brothers sell him as a slave and he ends up in Egypt.

After some major setbacks, Joseph comes to the aid of the pharaoh by explaining a dream that no one else can interpret.[h]

*Pharaoh said to Joseph, "I hereby put you in charge of the whole land of Egypt." Then Pharaoh took his signet ring from his finger and put it on Joseph's finger. He dressed him in robes of fine linen and put a gold chain around his neck. He had him ride in a chariot as his second-in-command, and men shouted before him, "Make way!" Thus he put him in charge of the whole land of*

*Egypt.*[i]

There is a famine in Egypt and Joseph's brothers come asking for food, not knowing that their brother is not only alive, but is now in charge. Joseph forgives them, and Jacob and his family move to Egypt permanently.

*Then Jacob left Beersheba, and Israel's sons took their father Jacob and their children and their wives in the carts that Pharaoh had sent to transport him. They also took with them their livestock and the possessions they had acquired in Canaan, and Jacob and all his offspring went to Egypt. He took with him to Egypt his sons and grandsons and his daughters and granddaughters — all his offspring.*[j]

---

[a] Genesis 12 to 14 (NIV)
[b] Genesis 21:1-3 (NIV)
[c] Genesis 22:1-19
[d] Genesis 24:1-67
[e] Genesis 25:19-34 (NIV)
[f] Genesis 26:1-5 (NIV)
[g] Genesis 32:22 to 33:30
[h] Genesis 39:1 to 41:57 (NIV)
[i] Genesis 37:1-36 (NIV)
[j] Genesis 42:1 to 47:31 (NIV)

# Chapter 4

As the years pass, the descendants of Jacob (known as Hebrews) become so many, that a later pharaoh decides to kill every Hebrew boy as soon as he are born. But pharaoh's daughter rescues a baby called Moses from the Nile, and brings him up in the royal palace.

*Now a man of the house of Levi married a Levite woman, and she became pregnant and gave birth to a son. . . . When she could hide him no longer, she got a papyrus basket for him and coated it with tar and pitch. Then she placed the child in it and put it among the reeds along the bank of the Nile. . . . Pharaoh's daughter went down to the Nile to bathe, and . . . she saw the basket among the reeds and sent her slave girl to get it. . . . "This is one of the Hebrew babies," she said. . . . She named him Moses, saying, "I drew him out of the water."* [a]

When he is a young man, Moses sees the Hebrews who are living in slavery now, and kills an Egyptian who is attacking a Hebrew. But Moses is being watched, and he has to flee to the land of Midian. Lack of space here prevents us looking in detail at what happens next, but God tells Moses to go back to Egypt and bring his people out of slavery, which he does.[b]

Now comes a major part of the red cord – God's rescue plan is still running with us. It comes four hundred years after Joseph was taken to Egypt as a slave, after being sold by his brothers, the sons of Jacob. God says that every Hebrew family – also called the Children of Israel (of Jacob), or Israelites – must kill a lamb or goat and wipe the blood over their door posts, to protect them from his anger in the coming night when God passes over. This will then be called the Passover, for obvious reasons, and will later become a picture for Christians of the blood of Jesus on the Cross sheltering them from God's judgment.

*Each man is to take a lamb for his family, one for each household. . . . Then they are to take some of the blood and put it on the sides and tops of the doorframes of the houses where they eat the lambs. . . . Eat it in haste; it is the LORD's Passover. On that same night I will pass through Egypt and strike down every firstborn — both men and animals — and I will bring judgment on all the gods of Egypt. I am the LORD. The blood will be a sign for you on the houses where you are; and when I see the blood, I will pass over you. No destructive plague will touch you when I strike Egypt.*[c]

Having fled from Egypt, the Israelites are wandering in a wilderness, short of food. It's not long before they begin to complain, and remember the "good times" in slavery.

*In the desert the whole community grumbled against Moses and Aaron. The Israelites said to them, "If only we had died by the LORD's hand in Egypt! There we sat around pots of meat and ate all the food we wanted, but you have brought us out into this desert to starve this entire assembly to death." Then the LORD said to Moses, "I will rain down bread from heaven for you." . . . So Moses and Aaron said to all the Israelites, "In the evening you will know that it was the LORD who brought you out of Egypt, and in the morning you will see the glory of the LORD, because he has heard your grumbling against him. . . . You are not grumbling against us, but against the LORD."* [d]

Which is exactly what happens. In the wilderness, God gives Moses the Ten Commandments,[e] with many rules and regulations for living in such hot and crowded conditions. The Israelites are close to the border of the land promised to Abraham — the Promised Land — but they are afraid to occupy it. Instead of trusting God, they make idols and worship them.

God instructs Moses to make a small ark (a box carried on poles) to contain the stones on which the Ten Commandments are written, and he also gives instructions on making a portable tent for sacrifice and worship.[f]

Racing on forty years, Moses is dead and his right-hand man

Joshua takes charge.

*After the death of Moses the servant of the LORD, the LORD said to Joshua son of Nun, Moses' aide: "Moses my servant is dead. Now then, you and all these people, get ready to cross the Jordan River into the land I am about to give to them — to the Israelites. I will give you every place where you set your foot, as I promised Moses."* [g]

Joshua prepares to occupy the land, but needs to know what lies ahead.

*Then Joshua son of Nun secretly sent two spies. . . . They went and entered the house of a prostitute named Rahab and stayed there. The king of Jericho was told, "Look! Some of the Israelites have come here tonight to spy out the land."*

*So the king of Jericho sent this message to Rahab: "Bring out the men who came to you and entered your house, because they have come to spy out the whole land."*

*But the woman had taken the two men and hidden them. . . . Before the spies lay down for the night, she went up on the roof and said to them, "I know that the LORD has given this land to you and that a great fear of you has fallen on us, so that all who live in this country are melting in fear because of you. . . . For the LORD your God is God in heaven above and on the earth below. Now then, please swear to me by the LORD that you will show kindness to my family, because I have shown kindness to you. Give me a sure sign that you will spare the lives of my father and mother, my brothers and sisters, and all who belong to them, and that you will save us from death."* [h]

Rahab is told to hang a red cord from her window when the Israelites come. The attacking Israelite soldiers will see the cord and keep the family safe. Our own red cord runs clearly through this episode, echoing the protection from the blood on the doorposts at the Exodus from Egypt with Moses, and foretelling the protection through death of Jesus in the New Testament.

*Then the two men started back. They went down out of the hills, forded the river and came to Joshua son of Nun and told him everything that had happened to them.*

*They said to Joshua, "The LORD has surely given the whole land into our hands; all the people are melting in fear because of us."*

Rahab the prostitute will become an ancestor of the great King David, and an ancestor of Mary the mother of Jesus. So Rahab, famous for her own red cord, has a major role in God's plans, and is an example of how God sometimes uses what seem to be the most unlikely and undeserving people.

Jericho falls (literally) and Rahab is kept safe. Having seen that they're on the winning side with God, you would think that the Israelites would be full of praise and worship. Instead, they start to follow the gods of the people they have conquered. After many setbacks, the Promised Land is finally divided among the twelve tribes, the descendants of Jacob, the Children of Israel.

*Now these are the areas the Israelites received as an inheritance in the land of Canaan, which Eleazar the priest, Joshua son of Nun and the heads of the tribal clans of Israel allotted to them.*[i]

Age catches up with Joshua, and he says farewell to the people he has led from the wilderness into the land that God promised to Abraham several hundred years earlier.

*"Be very strong; be careful to obey all that is written in the Book of the Law of Moses, without turning aside to the right or to the left. Do not associate with these nations that remain among you; do not invoke the names of their gods or swear by them. You must not serve them or bow down to them. But you are to hold fast to the LORD your God, as you have until now. The LORD has driven out before you great and powerful nations; to this day no one has been able to withstand you. One of you routs a thousand, because the LORD your God fights for you, just as he*

*promised. So be very careful to love the LORD your God."*[j]

If you've been observing how God's people often go wrong, you'll know what Joshua probably suspects will happen once they enter the Promised Land: the people will find the foreign gods, with their associated sex worship, to be extremely attractive.

*Then the Israelites did evil in the eyes of the LORD and served the Baals. They forsook the LORD, the God of their fathers, who had brought them out of Egypt. They followed and worshipped various gods of the peoples around them. They provoked the LORD to anger because they forsook him and served Baal and the Ashtoreths. In his anger against Israel the LORD handed them over to raiders who plundered them. He sold them to their enemies all around, whom they were no longer able to resist. Whenever Israel went out to fight, the hand of the LORD was against them to defeat them, just as he had sworn to them. They were in great distress.*[k]

---

[a] Exodus 2:11-15 (NIV)
[b] Exodus 3:1 to 6:12
[c] Exodus 12:1-13 (NIV)
[d] Exodus 16 (NIV)
[e] Exodus 20:1-17
[f] Exodus 36:1 to 40:38
[g] Joshua 1:1-3 (NIV)
[h] Joshua 2:1-24 (NIV)
[i] Joshua 14:1 to 21:45 (NIV)
[j] Joshua 23:1 to 24:33 (NIV)
[k] Judges 2:11-15 (NIV)

# Chapter 5

God calls a young man named Gideon to help his people.[a] After Gideon's death, various judges are called on, and one of the most famous judges is Samson.[b] More fighting and infighting follows Samson's dramatic death.

Later: *In the days when the judges ruled there was a famine in the land, and a man of Bethlehem in Judah went to sojourn in the country of Moab, he and his wife and his two sons.*[c]

We are about to run across the red cord again, because Naomi, the wife, is left a widow in the land of Moab, with both her sons also dead. One of her sons has married a local girl called Ruth. Ruth, although from Moab, and brought up to worship Moabite gods with the cult of child sacrifice, returns to Bethlehem with Naomi when the famine is over, and falls in love with one of Naomi's relatives, called Boaz.

*So Boaz took Ruth, and she became his wife. And he went in to her, and the LORD gave her conception, and she bore a son. Then the women said to Naomi, "Blessed be the LORD, who has not left you this day without a redeemer, and may his name be renowned in Israel!"*

Their descendants certainly did become famous. Ruth and Boaz are ancestors of King David, and of Mary the mother of Jesus. Rahab, a prostitute. Ruth, a woman from a country worshipping evil gods. Keep following the red cord.

Many years later, a woman called Hannah is praying for a child, and promises God that if she conceives, she will give the child to God.

*She said to her husband, "As soon as the child is weaned, I will bring him, so that he may appear in the presence of the LORD and dwell there forever."* [d]

The details are something you will have to read for yourself in 1 and 2 Samuel. Samuel is persuaded to give the people a king, much against his advice. Saul is chosen and anointed. But Saul does not turn out to be a good choice, and David, a shepherd boy subsequently anointed by Samuel, is standing by to take Saul's place. David kills the Philistine giant Goliath, and this makes Saul jealous rather than grateful.[e]

After the death of Saul, and under the rule of David, the twelve tribes live in relative harmony in their own territory, coming together to fight other nations as and when necessary.

Another distant ancestor of Mary comes onto the stage – Bathsheba. After committing adultery with Bathsheba, King David arranges to have her husband, Uriah, killed in battle. David and Bathsheba are both ancestors of Mary. With skeletons like Rahab, Ruth from Moab, and Bathsheba in the cupboard, it would have been easy for the writers of the Old Testament to leave out the embarrassing parts. The fact that names like these are included in the history of the Israelites, and also mentioned in the New Testament, is a clear indication of the reliability of what we read.

David, such an important person in God's plans, in spite of his many failures, is described by the apostle Paul as a man after God's own heart.[f] David wrote many of the Psalms in the Old Testament, but certainly not all of them. Some go back as far as the time of Moses. David's Psalms often centre on repentance.

David wants to capture Jerusalem, to make it God's city.

*The king and his men went to Jerusalem against the Jebusites, the inhabitants of the land, who said to David, "You will not come in here, but the blind and the lame will ward you off" – thinking, "David cannot come in here." Nevertheless, David took the stronghold of Zion, that is, the city of David.*[g]

David would like to build a permanent temple in Jerusalem, but because of his past life and the bloodshed in battle after battle, the prophet Nathan has to give David this message from God:

*I will give you rest from all your enemies. Moreover, the LORD declares to you that the LORD will make you a house. When your days are fulfilled and you lie down with your fathers, I will raise up your offspring after you, who shall come from your body, and I will establish his kingdom. He shall build a house for my name, and I will establish the throne of his kingdom forever.*[h]

The offspring referred to here is Solomon, one of David's sons from Bathsheba. Solomon was known as a wise king, and he gathered many proverbs in the book of that name.

*When David's time to die drew near, he commanded Solomon his son, saying, ". . . Keep the charge of the LORD your God, walking in his ways and keeping his statutes, his commandments, his rules, and his testimonies, . . . that the LORD may establish his word that he spoke concerning me, saying, 'If your sons pay close attention to their way, to walk before me in faithfulness with all their heart and with all their soul, you shall not lack a man on the throne of Israel.'"*[i]

Solomon, portrayed as the wisest king ever,[j] built the Temple in Jerusalem, saw the Queen of Sheba, and made many wise decisions. But eventually . . .

*Now King Solomon loved many foreign women . . . from the nations concerning which the LORD had said to the people of Israel, "You shall not enter into marriage with them, neither shall they with you, for surely they will turn away your heart after their gods." . . . When Solomon was old his wives turned away his heart after other gods, and his heart was not wholly true to the LORD his God, as was the heart of David his father. . . . Therefore the LORD said to Solomon, "Since this has been your practice and you have not kept my covenant and my statutes that I have commanded you, I will surely tear the kingdom from you. . . . Yet for the sake of David your father I will not do it in your days, but I will tear it out of the hand of your son."*[k]

Following the death of Solomon, the kingdom of the twelve tribes splits into two factions: ten tribes of Israel in the north with Samaria as their capital city; and two tribes of Judah and Benjamin in the south, with Jerusalem as their capital. Each country has a succession of their own kings, both good and bad.

In Israel, in the time of King Ahab, two mighty prophets, Elijah[l] and Elisha[m], perform great signs of God's power, but with little lasting effect. After the death of Elisha, God seems to give up on Israel, allowing the Assyrians to invade and finally capture the whole country, taking the people into captivity.

The red cord appears to be broken in the north, while in the southern kingdom of Judah the people mistakenly believe that God will protect them, no matter what they get up to. This is where the southern prophets play a major role.

Jeremiah is a major prophet in Judah, up to the fall of Jerusalem and the captivity by the Babylonians. He has a whole book of his prophecies and warnings in the Bible. Jeremiah tells the people that they are like an unfaithful wife, or children completely out of control, so judgment is inevitable — and the only thanks he gets for passing on God's message is imprisonment! However, he does have good news for the future, but for after 70 years in exile.

We can read about the troubles in Israel and Judah, with their kings and prophets, in the books of Kings and Chronicles.

---

[a] Judges 6:1 to 7:25
[b] Judges 13:1 to 16:31
[c] The whole book of Ruth (ESV quoted here)
[d] 1 Samuel 1:1 to 2:11
[e] 1 Samuel 17:1 to 19:24 (ESV)
[f] See Acts 13:22
[g] 2 Samuel 5:6-7 (ESV)
[h] 2 Samuel 7:11-13 (ESV)
[i] 1 Kings 2:1-4 (ESV)
[j] 2 Chronicles 1:1-13
[k] 1 Kings 11:1-12 (ESV)
[l] 1 Kings 16:29 to 2 Kings 1:18
[m] 2 Kings 2:1 to 13:25

# Chapter 6

When I started reading the Bible on my own, it took me a long time to understand how the accounts of the kings and prophets fitted together. The history of the kings is told in the books of Kings and Chronicles. The books of the prophets are listed together in our Bibles, and arranged in order of length or perceived importance, rather than date. Hence my (and maybe your) confusion. The books of the prophets cover the 300 or so years following the reign of Solomon, when there were the two kingdoms — large Israel in the north and smaller Judah with Benjamin in the south.

The prophet Amos spoke to both kingdoms around 767 to 753 BC, before Assyria invaded. Isaiah and Micah followed him in Judah, while Hosea was working in the northern kingdom. Their messages were that the people and their towns and cities would be destroyed unless they repented and turned back to God. How right they were.

Hosea is the last recorded prophet in Israel. The Assyrians, who have already captured much of Israel, sweep down on Samaria almost as soon as Hosea has finished preaching, destroying the city and taking the people captive. We don't hear much more about them. By the time of Jesus, the inhabitants are called Samaritans, despised by the Jews as being descended from Jewish and Assyrian stock, worshipping with a mixture of Jewish and pagan beliefs.

Modern Israel includes much of the land that became Judah and Israel after the reign of Solomon, which may cause some confusion when reading the Old Testament unless you are aware of this.

In the south, Isaiah and Micah were busy warning the people of Judah that they would suffer the same fate as neighbouring Israel if they didn't turn back to God. Over the next hundred or more years, sometimes they repented, sometimes they didn't. Some kings of Judah encouraged the worship of God, others were more interested in pagan gods. Their danger was to come not from the Assyrians, but from the emerging power of Babylon.

The prophets Nahum, Joel, Habakkuk and Zephaniah give clear warnings to the two tribes in Judah, which are ignored, and the final destruction of Jerusalem comes in 586 BC, at the end of the prophet Jeremiah's time. All except the poorest people are taken to Babylon. The prophet Ezekiel covers both the fall and the captivity. Daniel is one of the captives in what is known as the Exile.

The last king of Israel is Hoshea (c732-722 BC), and the last king of Judah is Zedekiah (c597-586 BC). Both kings are ruling when their countries fall to the invaders, but many years apart.

Hezekiah (729-686 BC) — you may remember him from the quiz in chapter one — is the fifth king of Judah after Solomon, during the time of the prophets Isaiah and Micah. You can read about the kings and prophets in the books of Kings and Chronicles, and of course about the prophets in the Old Testament books of their names.

Only one possible answer in the quiz about Hezekiah in chapter one is correct. He was indeed a wise king, one who did much to bring the people back to God, but ultimately foolish and selfish.

Hezekiah has to deal with the Assyrians, and pay them to leave his country alone. He consults the prophet Isaiah at this point. Here is a heavily abridged account of one of Isaiah's meetings with King Hezekiah. I urge you to read the whole reference, and not just this abridged portion. I have taken up the rest of the chapter with an account of Judah at this time, as it will help with understanding Bible history by discovering how real it is. Don't forget to imagine you're there, watching and listening. So what do you see and hear?

*In the fourteenth year of King Hezekiah, Sennacherib king of*

*Assyria came up against all the fortified cities of Judah and took them. And Hezekiah king of Judah sent to the king of Assyria at Lachish, saying, "I have done wrong; withdraw from me. Whatever you impose on me I will bear."*

*And the king of Assyria required of Hezekiah king of Judah three hundred talents of silver and thirty talents of gold. And Hezekiah gave him all the silver that was found in the house of the LORD and in the treasuries of the king's house.*[a] . . .

It seems that the payment is not enough to keep the Assyrians away. This message is shouted out in Hebrew below the walls of Jerusalem, so that everyone, not just Hezekiah, can hear and understand.

*"Hear the word of the great king, the king of Assyria! Thus says the king: 'Do not let Hezekiah deceive you, for he will not be able to deliver you out of my hand. Do not let Hezekiah make you trust in the LORD by saying, 'The LORD will surely deliver us, and this city will not be given into the hand of the king of Assyria.' . . . Has any of the gods of the nations ever delivered his land out of the hand of the king of Assyria?" . . .*

Hezekiah also gets the threat of invasion in writing:

*Hezekiah received the letter from the hand of the messengers and read it; and Hezekiah went up to the house of the LORD and spread it before the LORD. And Hezekiah prayed before the LORD and said: "O LORD, the God of Israel, enthroned above the cherubim, you are the God, you alone, of all the kingdoms of the earth; you have made heaven and earth. Incline your ear, O LORD, and hear; open your eyes, O LORD, and see; and hear the words of Sennacherib, which he has sent to mock the living God. Truly, O LORD, the kings of Assyria have laid waste the nations and their lands and have cast their gods into the fire, for they were not gods, but the work of men's hands, wood and stone. Therefore they were destroyed. So now, O LORD our God, save us, please, from his hand, that all the kingdoms of the earth may know that you, O LORD, are God alone."...*

*Then Isaiah the son of Amoz sent to Hezekiah, saying, "Thus says the LORD, the God of Israel: Your prayer to me about Sennacherib king of Assyria I have heard. . . . Therefore thus says the LORD concerning the king of Assyria: He shall not come into this city or shoot an arrow there, or come before it with a shield or cast up a siege mound against it. By the way that he came, by the same he shall return, and he shall not come into this city, declares the LORD. For I will defend this city to save it, for my own sake and for the sake of my servant David."*

*And that night the angel of the LORD went out and struck down 185,000 in the camp of the Assyrians. And when people arose early in the morning, behold, these were all dead bodies. Then Sennacherib king of Assyria departed and went home and lived at Nineveh.*

When he returns home, Sennacherib is assassinated by his sons. Later on, Hezekiah's pride is to lead to Jerusalem's eventual downfall. Although the Temple and royal palace have been stripped of much of their silver and gold to pay off the Assyrians, Hezekiah boasts about the remaining treasures in his palace, to a group of Babylonian officials on a state visit. How their eyes must have lit up.

*At that time Merodach-baladan the son of Baladan, king of Babylon, sent envoys with letters and a present to Hezekiah, for he heard that Hezekiah had been sick. And Hezekiah welcomed them, and he showed them all his treasure house, the silver, the gold, the spices, the precious oil, his armoury, all that was found in his storehouses. There was nothing in his house or in all his realm that Hezekiah did not show them.*

*Then Isaiah the prophet came to King Hezekiah, and said to him, "What did these men say? And from where did they come to you?"*

*And Hezekiah said, "They have come from a far country,*

*from Babylon."*

*He said, "What have they seen in your house?"*

*And Hezekiah answered, "They have seen all that is in my house; there is nothing in my storehouses that I did not show them."*

*Then Isaiah said to Hezekiah, "Hear the word of the LORD: Behold, the days are coming, when all that is in your house, and that which your fathers have stored up till this day, shall be carried to Babylon. Nothing shall be left, says the LORD. And some of your own sons, who shall be born to you, shall be taken away, and they shall be eunuchs in the palace of the king of Babylon."*

*Then said Hezekiah to Isaiah, "The word of the LORD that you have spoken is good." For he thought, "Why not, if there will be peace and security in my days?"* [b]

Hezekiah's desire to worship God did not rub off on his son Manasseh.

*And Hezekiah slept with his fathers, and Manasseh his son reigned in his place. Manasseh was twelve years old when he began to reign, and he reigned fifty-five years in Jerusalem. His mother's name was Hephzibah. And he did what was evil in the sight of the LORD, according to the despicable practices of the nations whom the LORD drove out before the people of Israel. For he rebuilt the high places that Hezekiah his father had destroyed, and he erected altars for Baal and made an Asherah, as Ahab king of Israel had done, and worshipped all the host of heaven and served them.*

*And he built altars in the house of the LORD, of which the LORD had said, "In Jerusalem will I put my name." And he built altars for all the host of heaven in the two courts of the house of the LORD. And he burned his son as an offering and used fortune-telling and omens and dealt with mediums and with necromancers. He did much evil in the sight of the LORD, provoking him to anger.*[c]

Manasseh's son Amon follows in his father's footsteps, but Amon's son Josiah reverses the evil of his father and grandfather, and restores much of the worship to God.[d]

Hezekiah was right in his wishful thinking that the destruction would not happen in his lifetime. It takes a hundred years for the whole of Judah to fall to the Babylonian army, culminating in the destruction of Jerusalem and the Temple in 586 BC[e], 136 years after the destruction of Samaria and Israel in the north. The people, apart from the very poor, are taken into exile in Babylon.

I have deliberately homed in on the story of Hezekiah. This should give a better idea of the problems in Israel and Judah in a snapshot of history, rather than giving the whole list of kings and their dates. There are nineteen recorded kings of Judah, plus one queen, after Solomon (c925-586 BC); and nineteen kings of Israel (c925-721 BC).

To dig deeper than this needs a larger book, and there are plenty of those available. The recorded accounts of the kings and prophets are intertwined in the Old Testament, even though their books in the Bible are not in chronological order. One way to knit them together is to find a reading plan that puts the Bible events in (probable) date order. A link to one such plan is at the start of this book, along with other recommended reading.

---

[a] 2 Kings 18:13 to 19:36 for the whole reading (ESV)

[b] 2 Kings 20:12–19 (ESV)

[c] 2 Kings 20:21 to 21:26 (ESV)

[d] 2 Kings 22:1 to 23:30

[e] 2 Kings 25:1-30

# Chapter 7

Kingdoms come and kingdoms go. And so it is with Assyria and Babylon. All through their captivity in Babylon, the people from Judah have been talking and singing about Jerusalem. Babylon eventually falls to the Persians in 539 BC. After 70 years in captivity, the people (mostly the children and grandchildren of the original captives) are allowed home, and given permission to rebuild the Temple in Jerusalem under the supervision of Nehemiah, with Ezra as the priest. The books of Nehemiah and Ezra cover this time, with Zechariah, Haggai and Malachi the prophets. So the red cord isn't broken after all, although at one stage it looked as though it had become badly frayed.[a]

*In the first year of Cyrus king of Persia, that the word of the LORD by the mouth of Jeremiah might be fulfilled, the LORD stirred up the spirit of Cyrus king of Persia, so that he made a proclamation throughout all his kingdom and also put it in writing: 'Thus says Cyrus king of Persia: The LORD, the God of heaven, has given me all the kingdoms of the earth, and he has charged me to build him a house at Jerusalem, which is in Judah. Whoever is among you of all his people, may his God be with him, and let him go up to Jerusalem, which is in Judah, and rebuild the house of the LORD, the God of Israel – he is the God who is in Jerusalem. And let each survivor, in whatever place he sojourns, be assisted by the men of his place with silver and gold, with goods and with beasts, besides freewill offerings for the house of God that is in Jerusalem.'*[b]

This is much to the dismay and hostility of the locals who have taken over the land. Nehemiah initially concentrates on restoring the protective wall around Jerusalem and joins Ezra in leading a religious revival.

*When Sanballat the Horonite and Tobiah the Ammonite servant heard this, it displeased them greatly that someone had come to seek the welfare of the people of Israel. So I went to Jerusalem and was there three days. Then I arose in the night, I and a few men with me. And I told no one what my God had put into my heart to do for Jerusalem.*

*There was no animal with me but the one on which I rode. I went out by night by the Valley Gate to the Dragon Spring and to the Dung Gate, and I inspected the walls of Jerusalem that were broken down and its gates that had been destroyed by fire. . . .*

*Then I said to them, "You see the trouble we are in, how Jerusalem lies in ruins with its gates burned. Come, let us build the wall of Jerusalem, that we may no longer suffer derision." And I told them of the hand of my God that had been upon me for good, and also of the words that the king had spoken to me. And they said, "Let us rise up and build."* [c]

The walls are eventually rebuilt and the Israelites start to live in peace. At the end of the book of the prophet Malachi in the Old Testament, the people of Judah are back in their own country, although under the authority of Persia and the Medo-Persian Empire. In Jerusalem, the Temple has been rebuilt, but it is much smaller than the one Solomon built. However, the people are united and waiting for the prophesied leader, the Messiah, to come to their aid.

Four hundred years pass before we come to the New Testament, and the only records of these years come from sources outside the Bible.

The Greeks had a great influence over that part of the world, and Alexander the Great conquers the country, now called Judea, but is persuaded not to destroy Jerusalem on his way south to invade Egypt in 332 BC.

Subsequently, a revolt led by Judas Maccabeus results in the Hasmonean dynasty of kings who ruled in Judea for over a hundred years. But in the first century BC, Rome will eventually take power, although Koine Greek (common Greek) has became the standard language, and will be the language of the New Testament writers. In 63 BC the Roman general Pompey attacks Jerusalem, and the whole country comes under the authority of Rome.

The Jews resent the Roman occupation, and are waiting for the Messiah who they now believe will form an army to deliver them from Rome. There are troubles from small groups of Jewish freedom fighters.

Pompey and the Roman Senate appoint Antipater as the Procurator of Judea, and make his two sons kings of Judea in the south, and Galilee in the north. The son who becomes king of Judea is Herod the Great. To appease the Jews, Herod builds them a new Temple. He is, however, disturbed by news from visitors from the east, who tell him that a new king has been born. Actually, he is terrified. Some Jews are causing him enough trouble as it is. Surely there is not to be a rival!

*Now after Jesus was born in Bethlehem of Judea in the days of Herod the king, behold, wise men from the east came to Jerusalem, saying, "Where is he who has been born king of the Jews? For we saw his star when it rose and have come to worship him." When Herod the king heard this, he was troubled, and all Jerusalem with him.*[d]

---

[a] Ezra 1:1-4 (ESV)

[b] Ezra 1:1-4 (ESV)

[c] Nehemiah 2.10-20 (ESV)

[d] Matthew 2:1-3 (ESV)

# Chapter 8

*For to us a child is born, to us a son is given; and the government shall be upon his shoulder, and his name shall be called Wonderful Counsellor, Mighty God, Everlasting Father, Prince of Peace.*[a]

This verse is not from the New Testament. It was written by Isaiah 700 years before the birth of Jesus, and is one of several prophesying the birth and death of Jesus. The Jews have been waiting for this child for centuries. The time has finally come.

*In the sixth month the angel Gabriel was sent from God to a city of Galilee named Nazareth, to a virgin betrothed to a man whose name was Joseph, of the house of David. And the virgin's name was Mary. And he came to her and said, "Greetings, O favoured one, the Lord is with you!"*

*But she was greatly troubled at the saying, and tried to discern what sort of greeting this might be.*

*And the angel said to her, "Do not be afraid, Mary, for you have found favour with God. And behold, you will conceive in your womb and bear a son, and you shall call his name Jesus. He will be great and will be called the Son of the Most High. And the Lord God will give to him the throne of his father David, and he will reign over the house of Jacob forever, and of his kingdom there will be no end."*

*And Mary said to the angel, "How will this be, since I am a virgin?"*

*And the angel answered her, "The Holy Spirit will come upon you, and the power of the Most High will overshadow you; therefore the child to be born will be called holy — the Son of God.*[b]

John an eyewitness, writes in one of his letters: *And we have seen and testify that the Father has sent his Son to be the Saviour of the world.*[c]

I cannot possibly summarise the life of Jesus in a couple of pages. I suggest you read one of the four Gospels, perhaps Mark for starters. Jesus grows up, and when he is about thirty years old he begins his ministry in his hometown, Nazareth.

*Jesus returned in the power of the Spirit to Galilee, and a report about him went out through all the surrounding country. And he taught in their synagogues, being glorified by all.*

*And he came to Nazareth, where he had been brought up. And as was his custom, he went to the synagogue on the Sabbath day, and he stood up to read. And the scroll of the prophet Isaiah was given to him.*

*He unrolled the scroll and found the place where it was written, "The Spirit of the Lord is upon me, because he has anointed me to proclaim good news to the poor. He has sent me to proclaim liberty to the captives and recovering of sight to the blind, to set at liberty those who are oppressed, to proclaim the year of the Lord's favour."*

*And he rolled up the scroll and gave it back to the attendant and sat down. And the eyes of all in the synagogue were fixed on him. And he began to say to them, "Today this Scripture has been fulfilled in your hearing." And all spoke well of him and marvelled at the gracious words that were coming from his mouth. And they said, "Is not this Joseph's son?"* [d]

As soon as Jesus points out that the Scriptures foretell *his* coming, this doesn't go down well when they realize he isn't a "famous" preacher from outside, but that he grew up in Nazareth.

*When they heard these things, all in the synagogue were filled with wrath. And they rose up and drove him out of the town and brought him to the brow of the hill on which their town was built, so that they could throw him down the cliff. But passing through their midst, he went away.*

Jesus is recorded in the Gospels as doing many miracles, teaching his Sermon of the Mount, and claiming to be the Messiah and the Son of God. He has many followers, and selects twelve to be his main disciples. There are three chapters in Matthew on the Sermon on the Mount.[e] You must read them for yourself. In the Gospels you can see how the red cord binds God's plan for rescue, in the life, death and resurrection of Jesus.

Eventually Jesus has upset the Jewish authorities too much, and they plan to kill him. This comes as no surprise to Jesus, for he says he came to die, to be a sacrifice for forgiveness of sins — our sins.

*"The Son of Man did not come to be served, but to serve, and to give his life as a ransom for many."* [f]

And so the plan comes into action. Jesus is arrested and tried before the governor Pilate. Pilate finds Jesus not guilty, but the Jewish leaders scream for him to be executed. Fearing a riot, Pilate hands Jesus over for crucifixion — the cruellest form of execution the Romans can devise.

*So when Pilate saw that he was gaining nothing, but rather that a riot was beginning, he took water and washed his hands before the crowd, saying, "I am innocent of this man's blood; see to it yourselves." And all the people answered, "His blood be on us and on our children!" . . .*

*Then the soldiers of the governor took Jesus into the governor's headquarters, and they gathered the whole battalion before him. And they stripped him and put a red robe on him, and twisting together a crown of thorns, they put it on his head and put a reed in his right hand. And kneeling before him, they mocked him, saying, "Hail, King of the Jews!" . . .*

*And when they came to a place called Golgotha (which means Place of a Skull), they offered him wine to drink, mixed with gall, but when he tasted it, he would not drink it. And when they had crucified him, they divided his garments among them by casting lots. . . .*

*The scribes and elders, mocked him, saying, "He saved others; he cannot save himself. He is the King of Israel; let him come down now from the cross, and we will believe in him. He trusts in God; let God deliver him now, if he desires him. For he said, 'I am the Son of God.'" . . .*

*Now from the sixth hour there was darkness over all the land until the ninth hour. . . . And Jesus cried out again with a loud voice and yielded up his spirit. And behold, the curtain of the temple was torn in two, from top to bottom. And the earth shook, and the rocks were split. . . . When the centurion and those who were with him, keeping watch over Jesus, saw the earthquake and what took place, they were filled with awe and said, "Truly this was the Son of God!" There were also many women there, looking on from a distance, who had followed Jesus from Galilee, ministering to him, among whom were Mary Magdalene and Mary the mother of James and Joseph and the mother of the sons of Zebedee.*[g] *. . .*

Joseph from Arimathea persuades Pilate to allow him to take the body of Jesus for burial in his own, previously unused, tomb.

*The next day, that is, after the day of Preparation, the chief priests and the Pharisees gathered before Pilate and said, "Sir, we remember how that impostor said, while he was still alive, 'After three days I will rise.' Therefore order the tomb to be made secure until the third day, lest his disciples go and steal him away and tell the people, 'He has risen from the dead,' and the last fraud will be worse than the first." Pilate said to them, "You have a guard of soldiers. Go, make it as secure as you can."*

---

[a] Isaiah 9:6 9 (ESV)
[b] Luke 1 (ESV)
[c] 1 John 4:14 (ESV)
[d] Luke 1 (ESV)
[e] Matthew 5:1 to 7:27
[f] Matthew 20:28 (ESV)
[g] Matthew 27:24-62 (ESV)

# Chapter 9

Guards and a heavy stone cannot seal the Son of God in a tomb. On the third day the tomb is empty. As he promised, Jesus has risen from the dead, on the first day of the week — the day we now call Sunday. Luke gives us more details in his Gospel.

*The women who had come with him from Galilee followed and saw the tomb and how his body was laid. Then they returned and prepared spices and ointments. On the Sabbath they rested according to the commandment. But on the first day of the week, at early dawn, they went to the tomb, taking the spices they had prepared. And they found the stone rolled away from the tomb, but when they went in they did not find the body of the Lord Jesus. While they were perplexed about this, behold, two men stood by them in dazzling apparel.*

*. . . The men said to them, "Why do you seek the living among the dead? He is not here, but has risen. Remember how he told you, while he was still in Galilee, that the Son of Man must be delivered into the hands of sinful men and be crucified and on the third day rise."*

*And they remembered his words, and returning from the tomb they told all these things to the eleven and to all the rest. Now it was Mary Magdalene and Joanna and Mary the mother of James and the other women with them who told these things to the apostles, but these words seemed to them an idle tale, and they did not believe them.*

*But Peter rose and ran to the tomb; stooping and looking in, he saw the linen cloths by themselves; and he went home marvelling at what had happened. . . .*

*As they were talking about these things, Jesus himself stood among them, and said to them, "Peace to you!"*

*But they were startled and frightened and thought they saw a spirit. And he said to them, "Why are you troubled, and why do doubts arise in your hearts? See my hands and my feet, that it is I myself. Touch me, and see. For a spirit does not have flesh and bones as you see that I have." And when he had said this, he showed them his hands and his feet. . . .*

*Then he opened their minds to understand the Scriptures, and said to them, "Thus it is written, that the Christ should suffer and on the third day rise from the dead, and that repentance and forgiveness of sins should be proclaimed in his name to all nations, beginning from Jerusalem. You are witnesses of these things."*

*He led them out as far as Bethany, and lifting up his hands he blessed them. While he blessed them, he parted from them and was carried up into heaven. And they worshipped him and returned to Jerusalem with great joy, and were continually in the temple blessing God.*[a]

Jesus is with his disciples and other friends for forty days before returning to heaven. The apostle Paul writes that more than five hundred people saw the risen Jesus on a single occasion, most of whom were still alive at the time he wrote about it.

*For I delivered to you as of first importance what I also received: that Christ died for our sins in accordance with the Scriptures, that he was buried, that he was raised on the third day in accordance with the Scriptures, and that he appeared to Cephas [Peter], then to the twelve. Then he appeared to more than five hundred brothers at one time, most of whom are still alive, though some have fallen asleep. Then he appeared to James, then to all the apostles. Last of all, as to one untimely born, he appeared also to me. For I am the least of the apostles, unworthy to be called an apostle, because I persecuted the church of God.*[b]

And this leads us on to the early Christian church where Paul, a strict Jewish Pharisee called Saul at the time, will shortly set out to eliminate all Christians. But he will be reckoning without the power of the Holy Spirit who is coming down on the disciples where they are meeting together.

*When the day of Pentecost arrived, they were all together in one place. And suddenly there came from heaven a sound like a mighty rushing wind, and it filled the entire house where they were sitting. And divided tongues as of fire appeared to them and rested on each one of them.*

*And they were all filled with the Holy Spirit and began to speak in other tongues as the Spirit gave them utterance. . . . And all were amazed and perplexed, saying to one another, "What does this mean?" But others mocking said, "They are filled with new wine."*

*But Peter, standing with the eleven, lifted up his voice and addressed them: "Men of Judea and all who dwell in Jerusalem, let this be known to you, and give ear to my words. For these people are not drunk, as you suppose, since it is only the third hour of the day. But this is what was uttered through the prophet Joel: "'And in the last days it shall be, God declares, that I will pour out my Spirit on all flesh, and your sons and your daughters shall prophesy, and your young men shall see visions, and your old men shall dream dreams; even on my male servants and female servants in those days I will pour out my Spirit, and they shall prophesy. And I will show wonders in the heavens above and signs on the earth below, blood, and fire, and vapour of smoke; the sun shall be turned to darkness and the moon to blood, before the day of the Lord comes, the great and magnificent day. And it shall come to pass that everyone who calls upon the name of the Lord shall be saved.'*

*"Men of Israel, hear these words: Jesus of Nazareth, a man attested to you by God with mighty works and wonders and signs that God did through him in your midst, as you yourselves know – this Jesus, delivered up according to the definite plan and foreknowledge of God, you crucified and killed by the hands*

*of lawless men. God raised him up, loosing the pangs of death, because it was not possible for him to be held by it."* [c]

Stephen is the first recorded Christian martyr, and Paul is present at his stoning outside the walls at Jerusalem, cheering the crowd on, and keeping watch on the coats of the killers.

*Stephen, full of grace and power, was doing great wonders and signs among the people. Then some . . . could not withstand the wisdom and the Spirit with which he was speaking.* [d]

Stephen tells the listeners about Jesus, but what he has to say makes some of the Jewish leaders angry. They do not want to hear that they have crucified the Son of God.

*Now when they heard these things they were enraged, and they ground their teeth at him. But he, full of the Holy Spirit, gazed into heaven and saw the glory of God, and Jesus standing at the right hand of God. And he said, "Behold, I see the heavens opened, and the Son of Man standing at the right hand of God." But they cried out with a loud voice and stopped their ears and rushed together at him. Then they cast him out of the city and stoned him. And the witnesses laid down their garments at the feet of a young man named Saul. And as they were stoning Stephen, he called out, "Lord Jesus, receive my spirit." And falling to his knees he cried out with a loud voice, "Lord, do not hold this sin against them." And when he had said this, he fell asleep.*

This is just the start of the persecution of Christians, something that is still happening in many countries today, where Christian are literally loosing their lives for their faith. But the red cord of rescue is holding fast.

*But Saul, still breathing threats and murder against the disciples of the Lord, went to the high priest and asked him for letters to the synagogues at Damascus, so that if he found any belonging to the Way, men or women, he might bring them bound to Jerusalem. . . . He approached Damascus, and sud-*

*denly a light from heaven flashed around him. And falling to the ground he heard a voice saying to him, "Saul, Saul, why are you persecuting me?" And he said, "Who are you, Lord?" And he said, "I am Jesus, whom you are persecuting. But rise and enter the city, and you will be told what you are to do."* [e]

Saul gets his new name of Paul, and his life is changed completely by this encounter with Jesus. He becomes one of the greatest Christian preachers and writers, travelling on missionary journeys, with others, to start churches all around the Mediterranean, and often returning to make sure they are growing in the faith. He also writes letters to these new churches, encouraging them — and even admonishing them when he hears disturbing news about some of the church members. We can read some of these letters (also known as epistles) in the New Testament today, along with some short(ish) letters from the apostles James, Peter, John and Jude.

The final book, Revelation, is a mix of warnings from God to seven churches that are not all they should be, with prophecies, visions, and promises for the future. This is probably the best known promise, where the other end of our red cord is anchored:

*"Behold, the dwelling place of God is with man. He will dwell with them, and they will be his people, and God himself will be with them as their God. He will wipe away every tear from their eyes, and death shall be no more, neither shall there be mourning, nor crying, nor pain anymore, for the former things have passed away."* [f]

---

[a] Luke 23:50 to 24:53 (ESV)

[b] 1 Corinthians 15:3-9 (ESV)

[c] Acts 2:1-24 (ESV)

[d] Acts 6:8 to 7:60 (ESV)

[e] Acts 9:1-31 (ESV) See also Acts 22:1-21 and Acts 26:1-23

[f] Revelation 21:1-4 (ESV)

# The Finishing Post

We will have managed to reach the finishing post in just 42 pages, the maximum allowed by the publisher! And the red cord is still tied firmly to that reassuring news in Revelation at the end of our last chapter. God's plan for us came good with the birth, death and resurrection of Jesus. We have been bought with a price — the blood of Jesus.

I have already included part of the book of Acts. In it, you can read how the first missionaries, filled with the Holy Spirit, set out to tell the good news of Jesus to the towns and cities around the Mediterranean. Life was hard and dangerous, and many of the apostles and others gave their lives for what they knew to be true. Here, Paul is leaving the members of the Ephesian church for the last time.

*I know that after my departure fierce wolves will come in among you, not sparing the flock; and from among your own selves will arise men speaking twisted things, to draw away the disciples after them. Therefore be alert, remembering that for three years I did not cease night or day to admonish everyone with tears. And now I commend you to God and to the word of his grace, which is able to build you up and to give you the inheritance among all those who are sanctified.*[a]

Paul and others are kept busy, visiting and writing letters to the new Christian churches. Some churches consist of Jewish converts where members, who want to continue the established Jewish traditions, try to force Gentile (non-Jewish) converts to adopt their practices.

Other churches are made up of gentile converts, where members are keeping a foot in the camp of their old religion. Others somehow get it right. It is to this mix of churches that the rest of the New Testament letters are written — and they are essential reading for Christians today. The teaching in the letters is powerful, and some of the most memorable promises in the Bible are in there. Be sure to read them.

Paul wrote the first series of letters in the New Testament, followed by the writing of other apostles, with the book of Revelation at the very end.

The book of Hebrews, near the middle of the New Testament letters, was written to Jewish converts to show them that Jesus was foretold in the Scriptures (our Old Testament — which is where our run through the Bible began) making it clear that the blood of animal sacrifices has been replaced once and for all by the blood of Jesus on the Cross — our red cord.

I am aware that I have had to leave out many, many important people, places and events, but to put them in 42 small pages would have resulted in a book consisting of little more than a long list, with sparse details. I want to show that the Bible is not a dusty old book that's difficult to understand. It's exciting and challenging, and very relevant for us today. Now, hopefully, when you read or hear about these missing names and events, you will be able to picture them in their correct timescale and location — while keeping an eye out for the red cord of God's salvation plan.

God speaks to us through the Bible. This quote from the apostle Paul, in a letter to his missionary friend Timothy, makes a memorable and powerful ending to this book:

*All Scripture is breathed out by God and profitable for teaching, for reproof, for correction, and for training in righteousness.*[b]

---

[a] Acts 20:17-38 (ESV)

[b] 2 Timothy 3:16 (ESV)

# About the Author

Chris Wright is married with three grownup children, and lives in the West Country of England where he is a home group leader with his local church. He has written many books, mostly for young readers. Here are Christian books currently in print with White Tree Publishing. Most titles are also available as e-Books in most formats.

**For family reading:**

*Mary Jones and Her Bible: An Adventure Book*
ISBN 978-0-9525-9562-5

*Pilgrim's Progress: An Adventure Book* ISBN 978-0-9525-9566-3

*Pilgrim's Progress — Special Edition* ISBN 978-0-9525-9567-0

*Zephan and the Vision* ISBN 978-0-9525-9569-4

*Agathos, The Rocky Island, and Other Stories*
ISBN 978-0-9525-9568-7

**For older readers:**

*So, What Is a Christian?* An introduction to a personal faith, a companion to this book. ISBN: 978-0-9927642-2-7

*Running Through the Bible* ISBN: 978-0-9927642-6-5

*Starting Out* – help for new Christians of all ages, a companion to this book
ISBN 978-1-4839-622-0-7
*English Hexapla — The Gospel of John* ISBN 978-0-9525-9561-8
Many adults enjoy *Pilgrim's Progress — Special Edition.*
(ISBN 978-0-9525-9567-0.) The story sticks closely to the events in John Bunyan's book and is set in that period, but Christian and Christiana are teenagers. A painless way to become familiar with the original!

**You can find further details on all these books on the websites of major internet booksellers and buy some titles from bookstores. Churches and Christian organizations worldwide can purchase multiple copies of *Starting Out, Help!, Running Through the Bible* and *So, What Is a Christian?* from the publisher.**

Made in the USA
Middletown, DE
19 June 2024

56048806R00027